Author Biographies

A. A. Milne
Revised Edition

Charlotte Guillain

Heinemann Library
Chicago, Illinois

www.capstonepub.com
Visit our website to find out more information about Heinemann-Raintree books.

To order:

☎ Phone 800-747-4992

💻 Visit www.capstonepub.com to browse our catalog and order online.

Edited by Rebecca Rissman, Daniel Nunn, and Sian Smith
Designed by Joanna Hinton-Malivoire
Picture research by Tracy Cummins
Production by Victoria Fitzgerald
Originated by Capstone Global Library Ltd

Library of Congress Cataloging-in-Publication Data
Guillain, Charlotte.
A. A. Milne / Charlotte Guillain.
p.cm.—(Author biographies)
Includes bibliographical references and index.
ISBN 9781484687529 (paperback)
ISBN 9781484687512 (ebook pdf)
1. Milne, A. A. (Alan Alexander), 1882-1956—Juvenile literature. 2. Authors, English—20th century—Biography—Juvenile literature. I. Title.
  PR6025.I65Z66 2012
  828'.91209—dc22   2011016058
  [B]

Acknowledgments
We would like to thank the following for permission to reproduce photographs: Alamy: CBW, 10, 23, CSU Archives/Everett Collection, 11, david hancock, 18, 23, Greg Balfour Evans, 5, PA Image, 9, Retro AdArchives, 13, Sergi Reboredo, 21, Stunning images, 7; AP Images: The Daily News, Maria Sestito, 20; Getty Images: Bettmann, 14, Bob Thomas/Popperfoto, cover, David Montgomery, 16, Evening Standard, 17, Heritage Images, 6, Hulton Archive, 4, 12, Mike Coppola, back cover, 15, 23, PA Images, 19; NARA: War & Conflict CD, 23 (war), Shutterstock Premier: RSM/Bournemouth News, 8; Shutterstock: Graeme Dawes, 23 (poem), Tatiana Popova, 23 (line drawing)

Every effort has been made to contact copyright holders of material reproduced in this book. Any omissions will be rectified in subsequent printings if notice is given to the publisher.

Disclaimer
All the Internet addresses (URLs) given in this book were valid at the time of going to press. However, due to the dynamic nature of the Internet, some addresses may have changed, or sites may have changed or ceased to exist since publication. While the author and publisher regret any inconvenience this may cause readers, no responsibility for any such changes can be accepted by either the author or the publisher.

Contents

Some words are shown in bold, **like this**. You can find them in the glossary on page 23.

Who Was A. A. Milne?

A. A. Milne was a writer.

He wrote stories and **poems** for children.

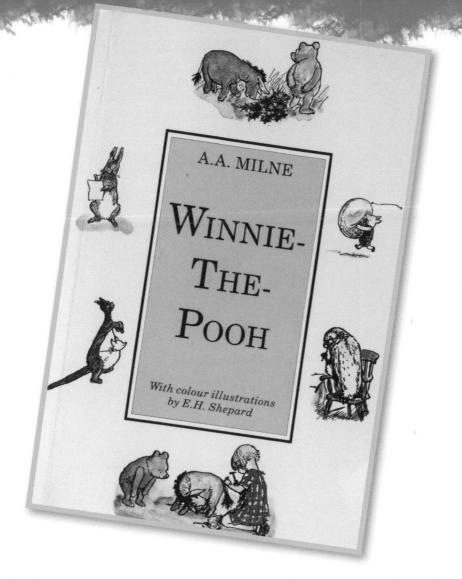

His full name was Alan Alexander Milne.

His most famous book is called
Winnie-the-Pooh.

Where Did He Grow Up?

A. A. Milne was born in 1882.

He lived in London, England.

Westminster School

A. A. Milne grew up in the school where his father was a teacher.

Then he went to a famous high school in London.

What Did He Do Before He Was a Writer?

World War 1 started in 1914.

A. A. Milne joined the army and went to fight in France.

After the war, A. A. Milne returned home to write **plays**.

Then he had a son called Christopher Robin.

How Did He Start Writing Books?

A. A. Milne wrote poetry for children that was **published** in magazines.

His **poems** were put together in a book called *When We Were Very Young*.

Then he wrote a book of stories called *Winnie-the-Pooh*.

Winnie-the-Pooh was Christopher Robin's stuffed toy bear.

What Books Did He Write?

A. A. Milne wrote two other books for children.

The House at Pooh Corner was also about Winnie-the-Pooh and his friends.

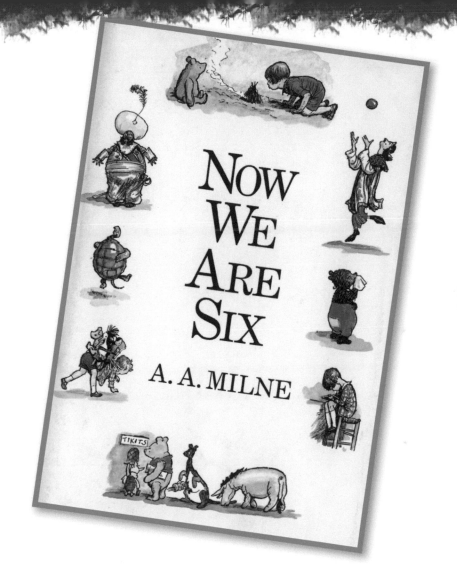

Now We Are Six was another **collection** of **poems**.

A. A. Milne also wrote some **plays** for adults.

What Did He Write About?

A. A. Milne's poetry was usually funny.

His **poems** were often about young children exploring the world.

A. A. Milne's stories were about his son Christopher Robin.

Christopher Robin's stuffed animals were also in these funny stories.

Who Drew the Pictures in A. A. Milne's Books?

A. A. Milne did not draw the pictures in his books.

Ernest H. Shepard was an artist who drew the pictures.

Some of Ernest's pictures are black and white **line drawings**.

Other pictures are painted in color.

What Else Did A. A. Milne Do?

A. A. Milne also wrote movies and **plays**.

He used the book *The Wind in the Willows* to write a play called *Toad of Toad Hall*.

A. A. Milne was not well when he got older.

He liked living in the country and reading books.

Why Is He Famous Today?

People still buy A. A. Milne's books today.

Many children see his characters in cartoon movies and on television.

You can see toys of these characters in the stores.

People still write books and magazines about them, too.

Timeline of A. A. Milne's Life and Work

1882   A. A. Milne was born in London.

1916   A. A. Milne went to France to fight in **World War 1**.

1920   Christopher Robin was born.

1924   *When We Were Very Young* was **published**.

1926   *Winnie-the-Pooh* was published.

1927   *Now We Are Six* was published.

1928   *The House at Pooh Corner* was published.

1956   A. A. Milne died.

Glossary

collection group of things put together

line drawing picture made of dark lines, done with a pen or pencil

play story that is acted out

poem piece of writing that puts ideas or feelings into words. Some poems rhyme.

published made into a book or put in a magazine and printed

World War 1 big war that lasted for more than four years

Find Out More

Books

Books by A. A. Milne and E.H. Shepard: *When We Were Very Young, Winnie-the-Pooh, Now We Are Six,* and *The House at Pooh Corner.*

Websites

www.poohcorner.com
Visit this website to find out more about A. A. Milne and Christopher Robin.

Index